Old Lurgan

with Waringstown and Moira

Rose Jane Leslie & Des Quail

Designed in the 1830s by Playfair, the renowned Edinburgh architect, Brownlow House was commissioned by Charles Brownlow MP who was made Baron Lurgan in 1839. The huge Tudor style house, standing next to Lurgan Park, contained 200 rooms and when the Brownlows lived there it was heated by open fires burning peat cut from the large tracts of bog land owned by the family. The family lived there until the 1890s before moving to England when the second Lord Lurgan married Lady Emily Cadogan. The house and land was bought by a local consortium before the Loyal Orange Orders bought the house in 1903 and presumably added the clock visible above the front door. Still the property of the Orange Order, Brownlow House remains the largest Orange lodge in the world. It has been attacked by bomb and fire more than once but substantial restoration work has been carried out and the house thrives as a venue for various meetings and events.

Text © Rose Jane Leslie, 2014.
Photographs from the Des Quail collection.
First published in the United Kingdom, 2014,
by Stenlake Publishing Ltd.
01290 551122
www.stenlake.co.uk

ISBN 9781840336856

**The publishers regret that they cannot supply
copies of any pictures featured in this book.**

Printed by
P2D Books, 1 Newlands Rd, Westoning, Bedford MK45 5LD

Further Reading

The books listed below were used by the author during her research. None of them are available from Stenlake Publishing. Those interested in finding out more are advised to contact their local bookshop or reference library.

Belfast and the Province of Ulster street directories.
County Armagh 100 Years Ago: A Guide and Directory, 1888, G.H. Bassett, republished 1989, Friar's Bush Press.
County Down 100 Years Ago: A Guide and Directory, 1886, G.H. Bassett, republished 1988, Friar's Bush Press.
Journals of the Craigavon Historical Society.
Lists of historic buildings, groups of buildings, areas of architectural importance in the area of the Craigavon falling within Moira rural district, Ulster Architectural Heritage Society, 1969.
Lists of historic buildings, groups of buildings, areas of architectural importance in the designated area of the Craigavon development commission, Ulster Architectural Heritage Society, 1970.
Lurgan: An Irish Provincial Town 1610–1970, Francis Xavier McCorry, 1993, based on PhD Thesis, 1986, Queen's University Belfast, published privately.
Lurgan Town Trail, Craigavon Historical Society.
The Lurgan Mail.

Distinguished by an Ionic doorcase, No. 40 Church Place, Lurgan, was built around 1750 by the Rev. Arthur Fforde, a cousin of the Brownlow family and rector of the parish church from 1748 to 1767. In the nineteenth and twentieth centuries the house became a convent school, but since 1996 has housed the Lurgan Credit Union.

Introduction

The foundation of Lurgan dates back to the 1610, during the Plantation of Ulster, when King James I granted John Brownlow and his son William, originally from Nottinghamshire, a total of 2,500 acres in the Barony of O'Neil, near the southern shore of Lough Neagh where the town now stands. Settling on their newly awarded land from 1611, the Brownlows also brought with them their families and other men including six carpenters, a mason, a tailor and six workmen. Six tenants and a free holder were also installed on this land, which was then mostly cattle pasture and bog. By 1619, as recorded in Pynnar's Survey, there was a bawn and a town of 42 houses situated on a ridge of land on which Lurgan's main street was eventually built.

In 1628 a patent was granted for a market and two fairs annually in what was then referred to as 'Ballylurgan'. The name is derived from several Irish versions: *an lorgain* (which means 'shin shaped hill'), *Lorgain Chlann Bhreasail* ('long ridge of Clanbrassil') or *Lorgain Bhaile Mhic Cana* (long ridge of McCann's townland). The latter was anglicised to 'Lurgivallivacket'. Old maps of the time suggest that the Brownlows built a bawn near the area between present day North Street and Windsor Avenue with the small dwellings of the English settlers adjacent. A parish church was built on the site of the present Shankill Graveyard. However, the initial period of settlement was disrupted by an attack on Lurgan during the 1641 rebellion by the McCanns, the Magennises and the O'Hanlons, all families dispossessed from the lands occupied by the Brownlows. William Brownlow, with his wife and children, were captured and imprisoned in Charlemont Fort for a period before they were released by Lord Conway's army and returned to Lurgan.

William Brownlow died in 1660, leaving no male heir. The Lurgan property passed to his grandson Arthur Chamberlain, who assumed the name of Brownlow upon inheritance. He founded a linen market and encouraged the production of linen on his estate by providing incentives such as granting awards for the best growth of flax and supporting the purchase of equipment. By 1708 the Lurgan area was a leading producer of fine linen cambric cloth. Skills of flax treatment, spinning and weaving were introduced by a number of Quaker families from the north of England who settled in Lurgan and the North Armagh area, while French Huguenots brought with them the craft of damask weaving for which the village of Waringstown nearby was particularly notable. Arthur Brownlow died in 1712 but his son William and descendants continued as the principal landowners.

By 1777 Lurgan had become a town of 400–500 houses. Meanwhile the William Brownlow of the day began to improve his estate and demesne, where a lake was dug and trees planted on the land which today is Lurgan Park.

The nineteenth century saw the fastest growth of Lurgan as a town, with the population leaping from 3,760 in 1836 to 8,500 by 1861. The trade in fine linen and hand woven cambric and damask continued to flourish until the mechanisation of weaving in the 1850s. Several power loom linen weaving factories were opened, such as the Lurgan Weaving Company in 1881, attracting many workers who further expanded the population to over 10,000, making it the fastest growing town in Ulster after Belfast. Other large linen factories included James Malcolm, Johnson Allen & Co. and Watson and Sons. Employment in Lurgan was also provided by handkerchief makers and hemstitching companies. The townscape had by then all of the churches, terraces and commercial buildings which characterise the town today, including Brownlow House built for the Charles Brownlow who was raised to the peerage as Baron Lurgan of Lurgan in 1839. The Ulster Railway on the Belfast to Dublin railway line extended to Lurgan in 1841, while the Lagan Canal was used to transport coal from Belfast to Lough Neagh and the Kinnego Cut just outside the town.

During the twentieth century demand for fine linen goods declined in the face of competition from cheaper and more varied fabrics and by the late 1950s Lurgan was no longer the manufacturing hub it had once been, although textile production continued until the late twentieth century in a much reduced form.

Another factor that would affect Lurgan was the introduction of Craigavon in 1965, a new town intended to incorporate Lurgan with the neighbouring town of Portadown to form a linear city. Lurgan council and court were transferred to a site between the two towns under the umbrella of Craigavon Civic Centre and a large shopping precinct has also grown around this, unfortunately taking custom away from Lurgan town. Though the distinctive long, wide main street remains, the town is a shadow of the industrial hub that thrived 100 years ago.

The gate lodge at the entrance to Lurgan Park in Windsor Avenue was designed by Henry Hobart in 1908, appointed by Lurgan Urban Council who had paid £2,600 to the Lurgan Real Property Company in 1907 for 73 acres to use as a public park. The lodge is built in red brick to an attractive Edwardian design with a fanlighted front door and diamond pane windows; the cost of its execution was £300. Lurgan Park was opened officially on 31 July 1909 by the Earl of Aberdeen KP, Lord Lieutenant of Ireland, and the Countess of Aberdeen. Today it is one of the largest urban parks in the United Kingdom.

A crowd gathered in Church Place, surrounding the Earl and Countess of Aberdeen as they arrive to officially open Lurgan Park in July 1909. On the day the dignitaries arrived from Dublin by train at midday and were driven to Lurgan Park for the opening ceremony. They cannot be seen here, but are somewhere in the centre of a crowd. The event was one of great civic importance as fresh air and the open space of a town park was seen as important for the health of local citizens, especially factory workers, and as a combatant against tuberculosis which was prevalent at the time. On the day a special guard of honour of the Boys Brigade and Church Lads was formed at the park entrance which was decorated with flags and an arch. Shops were closed and factory workers finished at 11 a.m. so that plenty could witness the programme of events that included numerous speeches, music, a lunch and a demonstration by school children. Some received gifts from Lady Aberdeen – silver thimbles for the girls and autograph books for the boys. The proceedings were covered at length in the *Lurgan Mail*, the day described as one which would 'long rank as a most auspicious day in the pages of Lurgan's history'.

A game of cricket in progress in Lurgan Park in 1909. Cricket had been played in the parkland since the 1850s by the Lurgan Demesne Cricket Club. The Brownlow family had for many years allowed local people to use the parkland which is a short walk from the town centre. In the 1880s the club had 40 members who paid a subscription of 10 shillings a year.

Brownlow Park contains a large lake which was dug out during the eighteenth century in what had been poor, boggy land. There is a theory that the expression 'long as a Lurgan spade', meaning to look unhappy, originates from the time when low paid labourers toiled at digging the lake. Over time, the purpose of the lake became chiefly ornamental, but in the late eighteenth century when it was first dug there was a dam at the northern end which drove a cornmill belonging to the Brownlow family. At that time there was also a windmill. Trees were planted in clumps and avenues to improve the view and a high wall was built around the perimeter of the park.

Market St. Lurgan

A market day around 1911, the year of the completion of the Ulster Bank, the large building on the right with two gables. There had been a market in Lurgan since 1629 when a patent was granted for a market on Fridays and two fairs on the feast of St James and the feast of St Martin. The trade of linen predominated and by 1780, as noted by Arthur Young during his tour of Ireland, the linen market had a weekly turnover of £5,250 a week. As noted in *Bassett's Directory and Guide to Co. Armagh*, market day was changed from Friday to Thursday around 1848 to avoid a clash with the Friday market in Belfast which was attended by all the manufacturers and linen merchants throughout Ulster. After power loom weaving was introduced in 1855 the linen markets declined and the linen hall built near the church was demolished in 1865. In Lurgan the Thursday market continued into the twentieth century for the sale of grain, grass seed in season, pork, fowl, butter, eggs, hay, straw and potatoes etc. On Saturday there was also a market for fresh meat.

Robert John Welch, one of Northern Ireland's most prolific and important early photographers took this picture on High Street in 1904. The double storey house with the roof removed was demolished to be replaced by a new post office building. Herbert's Market, to the left, was set up by Joseph Herbert who came from Lithuania to settle in Lurgan in the late 1880s. As described by local historian F.X. McCorry, Mr Herbert, who was Jewish, founded a small community of co-religionists for whom he provided work as travellers and collectors. By 1903 it was large enough to have a house of worship and Hebrew school in North Street. The congregation lasted only 20 years due to its small number, remembered as about 15 families at the most, and declined after Mr Herbert died in about 1922.

Market Street looking up High Street around 1905, after the new post office building with the rounded gable on the left was constructed. The post office was at No. 2 Market Street; in 2011 it was reinstated on the same site, although the building in the picture had been long since demolished. Notice the dirt surface of the street where lumps of dung and a cart track can be seen. Before the days of tarmac, in dry weather the road became very dusty, a problem that was alleviated with the use of a watering cart for which the town council was responsible. The roads were surfaced with rough stones, which required rolling, a recurrent subject in the Lurgan Urban District Council agenda of the early 1900s. In the distance there appears to be a crowd on High Street, perhaps relating to one of the many public meetings that were reported in the *Lurgan Mail*.

(R.I.C. Royal Irish Constabulary, the Irish Police Force before the two Parliaments)

Ivy Lodge, R. I. C., Lurgan

By 1907 Ivy Lodge in Church Place had become the principal Royal Irish Constabulary station in Lurgan. There were two other police stations in Queen Street and Edward Street. The local constabulary then consisted of about 30 men and for a time the head constable would have lived with his family upstairs. Ivy Lodge, built in 1810, was destroyed by an IRA bomb in 1973. A new police station was erected in approximately the same place and remains there today.

In 1910 David Pedlow's shop at No. 43 Church Place was a spirit merchant and, according to his advert, purveyor of 'building materials of every description; timber, sewer pipes, gully traps, tiles, alabaster, cement, fire blocks, slates, corrugated iron, laths, sand, mortar, lime and putty'. The premises, in which the family lived upstairs, were burnt in February 1902 and perhaps this photograph was taken to mark the refurbishment of the business. By 1918 Pedlow had become a motor agent and left Church Place in the years following. By 1939 E. Pedlow was trading in William Street as a cycle agent.

At some 50 metres Market Street is regarded as the widest street in Ireland and is one of Lurgan's defining features. From the eighteenth century until the end of the nineteenth century there was another row of buildings down the centre of Market Street, known as Middle Row. These included a Market House with an upstairs courtroom, which was burnt down in 1776 but replaced further down the row. Other houses and shops were added but were eventually demolished.

The Church of Ireland Shankill Parish, the Church of Christ the Redeemer at the end of the nineteenth century. The wooden structure in Church Place, at the left of the picture, was a remnant of the old Middle Row which stood in the centre of Market Street until the late 1890s. The church was consecrated in 1725, built on what had been the town 'Green' to replace an earlier church sited at the old Shankill Graveyard where a place of worship had existed since the time of the plantation. It was built in two main phases, in 1725 and 1863, with a further enlargement in 1931. Stones from the original Shankill Church were used to build the steeple. Inside there is a font bearing the date 1684, also taken from the old church. The substantial terrace with four houses behind the church was built in 1885 by Arthur Donnelly with funds accumulated by a successful spirit grocery business at 50 Church Place.

Church Place, probably in the 1920s after the war memorial was added looking in the direction of William Street. On the right there is a handsome gas lamp. Gas lighting was introduced to Lurgan in 1857 with 67 lamps. More were added in 1861 and in the 1880s. The high building with a circular window in the gable end at No. 8 Church Place, The Cinema, was built in 1913 but the cinema on the ground floor was burnt in 1921 and in the 1930s and 40s was used as an indoor market.

The official unveiling on 23 May 1928 of the Lurgan war memorial, built to commemorate over 300 men from the Lurgan area killed in the First World War. The ceremony was carried out by the Governor of Northern Ireland, the Duke of Abercorn, whose other ceremonial duties within the same week included laying a foundation stone for Parliament Buildings at Stormont. The names of the fallen from the First World War are inscribed on the central pillar. After the Second World War the names of some 81 soldiers were added. Today there is also a memorial to members of the UDR killed in the troubles in the form of a small stone obelisk on the plinth. The bronze winged figure represents the spirit of peace.

Market Street, showing War Memorial, Lurgan.

Another view of Market Street, this time looking towards Shankill Church, probably from the late 1920s. Behind the rear of the bus on the left can be seen the balustraded parapet of the Bank of Ireland, a converted shop premises with a simple classical facade. Opposite, behind the telegraph pole, is the more grandiose Ulster Bank with gables and a pillared entrance which was purpose built in 1911. The telegraph poles are conspicuous; Lurgan's connection with the outside world by electric telegraph was made in the 1850s.

The Lurgan Weaving Factory Limited (with Brownlow House in the background) was established in 1881, having been bought over from William and James Macoun who had manufactured cambric and cambric handkerchiefs there since the 1860s. The new factory, sometimes called the Lake Factory or 'the Limited', had 472 looms to weave products which were then sold unbleached to merchants in Lurgan, Belfast and elsewhere in Northern Ireland. On the board of directors were Samuel and Frederick Bell, Thomas A. Dickson MP of Dublin, James Brown JP of Donaghmore, Co. Tyrone, and H.G. Macgeagh of Derry Lodge, Lurgan. The firm flourished, securing a large overseas market for fine handkerchiefs. It was later taken over by the Blackstaff Spinning and Weaving Co. Ltd but eventually closed down in 1967.

Lurgan linen factory workers assembled during the Weavers' and Winders' Strike which took place over five weeks during January and February 1913. From 1911 trade union membership had increased in Lurgan to enable an organised protest against low wages, which had remained static since the 1880s despite increasing living costs. The winders also complained about the poor quality of yarn they had to use which resulted in lower quality cloth for which they were paid less. During the strike the four main linen factories closed down. These were the Lurgan Weaving Co. Ltd, Messrs Malcolm Ltd, Messrs Johnson Allen and Co. and Mr W.J. Allens' factory. An estimated 6,000 people, about half the population of Lurgan at the time, were affected. The majority of those on strike were weavers, while there were about 200 winders, mostly women. While the weavers ceased work during the strike, the winders were employed with outwork from the hemstitching factories in the town. Eventually a compromise was reached when the union accepted a modest wage increase from the factory owners, which was less than the farthing a yard for output of material that the strikers had wanted.

Edward Street from the corner of Church Place in the 1920s. The car on the left, perhaps a bull nosed Morris Cowley, is parked in front of a public house. Both the public house and the building opposite have changed little but the terraced houses on the left at Convent Row were demolished on the late 1960s to make way for a new road and junction that sweeps traffic to the left on to what is now Millenium Way.

Edward Street, across the road from the convent in the 1930s, with Matt Tipping's grocer's shop at the corner of Shankill Street. The Tipping family ran a grocery business from various different premises in Edward Street for at least 50 years.

William Street, showing the distinctive arched chimney and Doric arched doorway of the old courthouse. Built of yellow brick, it was designed in 1873 and continued in use until 1973 when the Craigavon Crown Court was created. The courthouse is now a public house. Just beyond, at the intersection with Charles Street, is a memorial that commemorates the Rev Thomas Millar, minister of Lurgan First Presbyterian Church from 1844 to 1858, who died, aged 38, in the Trent Valley rail disaster. The spire of the parish church is in the background of the photograph.

Construction of St Peter's Roman Catholic Church in North Street started in 1832 on a site granted by Charles Brownlow after the Catholic Relief Act of 1800. Before 1800, as stated in Bassett's *County Armagh*, Roman Catholics had nowhere to worship in Lurgan and had to congregate in a shed in Tanaghmore townland about a mile outside the town. St Peter's Church was dedicated in 1833 but was enlarged twice, in 1869 and 1897, to accommodate the growing congregation. The tower was added later and dedicated in 1901. Reaching a height of almost 200 feet, it is Lurgan's tallest structure.

A large Orange arch, constructed at the town end of Lough Road not far from the railway station, to celebrate the Twelfth of July during the 1920s.

Lurgan Station opened in 1841 and connected Belfast Great Victoria Street to Portadown and Armagh. The station building shown here is a close replica in design to the one of Lisburn which dates from 1878. The latter has been preserved, but Lurgan's old station building was damaged by a bomb in 1972 and a modern replacement building was completed in about 1981.

The Model School building, in Brownlow Terrace overlooking the railway, was finished in 1863 at a cost of £6,000 and could accommodate 600 pupils in three departments for boys, girls and infants. The curriculum included reading, geography, arithmetic, book keeping, music, physical science and chemistry. Also provided at the school were night classes for young men and boys who were employed during the day. Model schools were non-denominational establishments built in each county and were so named because they served as an example to other national schools and were used for the training of teachers. Today the building is the Lurgan Model and Primary School Unit. This photograph dates from 1897.

Due to the rising number of motor vehicles on the roads, by the 1940s the central reservation of Market Street had been demarcated as parking space. A branch of Woolworths 3 and 6d stores had taken up residence in the lower floor of the Brownlow Arms Hotel. The Brownlow Arms has been in existence as a hotel since the 1840s and continues today as a public house, though the original building was rebuilt after a 1000lb car bomb damaged much of this stretch of Lurgan's High Street in 1992.

High Street, with the Methodist Church third on the left with the rounded upper windows and a balustrade on the roof. It was built in 1826 but remodelled in 1888 when the balustrade was added (it has since been removed). The presence of Methodism in Lurgan dates from the time of John Wesley in 1767 when he visited the town and was received by Mr Millar, father of Joseph Millar (of the Millar memorial in William Street). The square tower beyond belongs to the Mechanics' Institute. First on the left is the former Greyhound Hotel, once a posting house on the stage route from Belfast to Armagh. Opposite, immediately on the right are Nos. 42–46 High Street, described by C.E.B. Brett as 'a splendid blackstone three storey block of around 1810 ... with excellent crisp stucco mouldings upstairs'. Today it is much lightened in appearance by the application of pale grey paint.

On the near right, at the top of Union Street, is a side view of the Mechanics' Institute on Market Street. Opened in 1858, this was one of about 300 such establishments throughout Britain and Ireland that were initiated by George Birbeck, a Yorkshire philanthropist, to enable those employed in factories and elsewhere to receive a scientific education as a means of 'aiding their practical skill, by the elucidation of science and of calling forth the energies of their minds to Invention and Improvement'. The institute therefore contained a library, with rooms for reading and evening classes. Beside the institute was the town hall, built in 1868 and now used as an arts centre. Just beyond it was a police station in the early 1900s. Modern development has altered the much of the rest of Union Street where also was once found the workhouse, now a hospital site.

Uprichard's Home Furnisher and Ironmongery on High Street in the 1920s, with a great many large bowls on display in the window. Uprichard traded in the High Street until the 1970s.

High Street in 1907, taken close to the First Presbyterian Church. Characteristic of the street are the substantial town houses such as those immediately on the right. Each house or block had its own gateway leading to yards in which were often kept dairy cows or pigs. There were a number of urban farms in Lurgan; the last to exist was as late as the 1960s. About half way down on the right beyond the telegraph pole can be seen the gable of the then newly built Belfast Banking Company which was completed in 1902. Close by is the point where a statue of the celebrated greyhound Master McGrath is now placed, which bears the inscription 'presented in 1993 by Major William Brownlow and Mr Jamie Brownlow on the return of McGrath to Ireland after 100 years.'

Master McGrath was one of most successful greyhounds of his time. Owned by Lord Lurgan, Master McGrath won the Waterloo Cup in 1868, 1869 and 1871. Born in County Waterford, as a puppy he seemed to have little promise as the runt of the litter, but he turned out to be powerfully built, his potential being recognised by the boy who looked after him and after whom the dog was named. A terrace of houses near the Walthamstow greyhound racing track in London was built from his winnings and his story also inspired a ballad of eleven verses. Master McGrath died of heart disease on Christmas Eve, 1873. Owing to a suspicion that the dog had been poisoned an autopsy was carried out which revealed that his heart was twice the size of a normal dog's heart. A description of the time relates that Master McGrath was buried ceremoniously in an oak coffin while members of the Brownlow household staff looked on. This memorial statue was photographed in the grounds of Brownlow House but was later taken to Culford Hall at Bury St Edmunds, family home of Lady Emily Cadogan following Lord Lurgan's marriage in 1894. There is another memorial to Master McGrath outside Dungarvan, County Waterford.

The First Presbyterian Church on High Street dates from 1828. The classical portico was added in 1860, though the congregation is much older, having been established in Lurgan in 1688 when a meeting house on the other side of the street was used. Inside there is a large gallery and seating accommodation for 1,000 people. The foundation stone was laid by Mr Charles Brownlow, later Lord Lurgan. The first minister at this church was the Rev. Hamilton Dobbin, incumbent until 1844. His successor, the Rev. Thomas Millar, helped to found a school house behind the church but died relatively young and is commemorated by a memorial monument outside the old court house in William Street.

A school party outside what is probably the former school house in Queen Street in the early 1900s. The horse drawn wagonette was hired from the Kennedy firm in Lurgan. Such vehicles tended to be bought new by the gentry and the better off before being sold to a vehicle hire company for use as an old fashioned equivalent of a minibus today.

Little remains today of the buildings in this part of Queen Street, seen here looking towards the outskirts of town in the early 1900s. The substantial building in the right foreground has been demolished as has the large house with three chimneys on the left near the top of the hill. Part of the two storey terraces do remain but a great deal of the housing has been renewed, considerably altering the view. The sapling, just visible on left, has however continued to grow and is now at the top of a line of trees that stretches along this road.

Scott's grocer's shop in Queen Street, around 1911, probably with the proprietor, Thomas J. Scott, who was established there in business by 1910. Street directories indicate that the business continued in these premises until the 1940s. Mr Scott seems to have followed a family trade of long standing: an entry in the 1848 *Slater's Directory* lists a John Scott, provision merchant of Back Lane.

Queen Street in the 1920s, looking in the direction of High Street. At No. 104, by the junction with King Street, is Harrison Campbell's grocer's shop, which was listed in the 1926 Business Directory of Ireland published in the *Macdonald's Irish Directory and Gazetteer*. The premises are now taken by a musical instrument shop.

Beyond Queen Street begins Avenue Road which was named after the old avenue to Brownlow House which was behind the trees on the left. The long row of low buildings beyond was part of James Allen's factory, listed as a damask manufacturer and jacquard machine maker in Bassett's 1886 County Armagh Directory.

The junction of Flush Place with Queen Street, looking out towards the Banbridge Road. The road is named after the Flush River or, as some locals call it, 'the flushing' which flows adjacent to the row of cottages on the left. Also sited here was a hand loom factory founded by Francis Watson in 1808, possibly one of the earliest such factories in Ireland. The cottages, built for the factory workers, are also attributed to Watson. As discussed by historian F.X. McCorry, contemporary records indicate that in 1831 Watson was responsible for the construction of some 23 workers' cottages. His factory, by then trading as Robert Watson (Lurgan) Ltd, continued to manufacture handkerchiefs until the 1950s. Today the cottages on the left have gone and the area is redeveloped with commercial premises. Also demolished at some time in the last 40 years is the traditional thatched cottage in the left foreground which was noted in the Ulster Architectural Society's List of 1968 as being 'in reasonably original condition'. The gable end to the right belongs to a gospel hall that, according to a street directory, was still in evidence in 1959 but had disappeared 10 years later. By 1972 another gospel hall had been established in Malcolm Road where a property on Bengal Terrace was bought by the brethren.

The large pillars on the right belong to the residence of George Rogers JP, listed as a farmer living at the Demesne which by 1918 was renamed Windsor Lodge. New houses have since been built there although the area continues to be known by the older name. Waringstown is named after William Waring who in 1656 bought land from Cromwellian soldiers. Originally the land belonged to the Magennis clan, Lords of Iveagh, whose property was forfeited for their part in attacking Lisburn in 1641 and then redistributed to soldiers. By around 1770 Waring had established a bleach green that employed English settlers in the manufacture of linen. In 1851 the company won a British Empire gold award for linen production. In the late nineteenth century some 300 to 400 handloom weavers lived in the village, working in cottages such as these which were built to accommodate a 'shop' that was equipped with a hand loom. Many of these weavers were immigrants of Huguenot origin. In the 1800s Waringstown also had a brewery and other clothing factories.

The loom shown here, photographed in Waringstown, was of the Jacquard type used to weave fine damask cloth. The word damask, which means 'beautiful cloth' is thought to originate from the language of the Phoenicians who traded it for tin from Cornwall. This particular loom was used for making damask napkins. Waringstown weavers produced hand woven damask of world famous quality and for the coronation of King George II produced a remarkable table cloth which measured 11 feet by 9, bearing woven illustrations of the coronation procession, the royal arms and a map of London. The cloth can be seen today at the Lisburn Linen Museum. Linen weaving in Waringstown continued until 1968 when the John McCollum firm closed down. Hand woven linen was still produced there in the early twentieth century in the teeth of competition from machine weaving, to the extent that in 1909 the Waringstown weavers asked for legislation for their cloth to have 'hand woven linen damask' incorporated in the fabric to distinguish their product from power loom cloth.

A Damask Napkin Handloom Weaver, Warringstown.

Waringstown War Memorial

The Waringstown War Memorial under construction in 1919/20, a monument instigated by Mrs Waring whose husband, Lieutenant Colonel Holt Waring, was killed in action in April 1918. Holt's brother, Lieutenant Commander Ruric Waring, was killed at sea in October 1914 when the HMS *Hawke* was hit by a torpedo. The memorial consists of a Gothic renaissance style clock tower that stands 40 feet high in the village on the Banbridge Road. It was designed by the architect Robert Lynn of Lurgan and Belfast. A number of other Waringstown men were killed in the First Word War and the memorial, funded by public subscription, also commemorates those who fell in the Second World War.

Moira Orange Hall, at the top of the Main Street, as it was in the early twentieth century. A date stone in the wall is marked 'Deramore Orange Hall, 1904'; it was named after Thomas Bateson who was elevated to the peerage as Lord Deramore in 1885. Over the years the building was used as a temporary hall by churches, such as St John's Church in the 1960s, before a new parochial hall was built, and by the Baptist Church who met there during the 1980s. At present a nursery playgroup is run in the building.

The village of Moira, four miles outside Lurgan, seen in 1923 with the police station to the left. The main street was laid out in the eighteenth century and remains noteworthy owing to the number of original Georgian buildings, mostly built between 1770 and 1830, that survive. The distinctive market house at the end of the street, partly obscured by lime trees, was completed in 1810 by the Bateson family who bought Moira from the Earls of Rawdon in the early 1800s. The building, which still bears the Bateson coat of arms, contained a large assembly room and a court room. The four lime trees in the centre, one of Moira's distinctive features, were eventually cut down but replanted in the late 1960s.

The National School in the early twentieth century, soon after its opening in 1903. The construction was supervised by Mr J.L. Dowie, land steward of the Deramore estate, and it replaced an earlier school built by the previous landlords, the Earls of Rawdon. By then the process of selling off the Deramore estate had begun following the death of Lord Deramore (born Thomas Bateson) in 1895. Since acquiring Moira in the early nineteenth century, the Batesons tended their Moira property from a distance as they lived at Belvoir Park outside Belfast throughout the period of ownership. When another primary school was built elsewhere in the village in the 1970s, the old schoolhouse was transferred to St John's Church as directed by a charter which stated that when the building ceased to be used as a school it should be returned to the church.

Moira Main Street from the Market House end. The house immediately to the left is still residential. Next door is Job Palmer's shop and beside it Turkington's blacksmiths. Nearby to this part of Moira, also known as Palmer's Corner after the shop, was a brewery and bottling plant although Moira was renowned chiefly as a centre for limestone quarrying. In the 1830s the Ordnance Survey Memoirs noted the activity of cotton muslin weaving there for the Glasgow Company. Thread was sent from Belfast and the muslin fabric made in Moira was then sold abroad. During the nineteenth century Moira remained a small village as there was no significant participation in the linen trade, unlike in other towns such as Lurgan. During the late twentieth century Moira has grown as a commuter town thanks to rail links and the proximity of the M1 motorway constructed in the 1960s.

PARISH CHURCH - MOIRA.

Construction of St John's Church of Ireland, the parish church in Moira, started in 1722 on a site given by the Hill family, at that time the owners of ground opposite Moira Castle. According to one tradition there was a tunnel that ran from the castle, which is long since demolished, to the church. The church was consecrated in 1723 and has been in continuous use since then. In 1884 the church steeple blew down and was eventually replaced by one made of copper. In this photograph of 1911 the steeple appears to be missing and is represented by lines drawn on to the print, which suggests that the picture was taken while the church lacked a steeple for a surprisingly long period.

According to Samuel Lewis's topographical memoirs of 1830, the rectory at Moira, also seen here in 1911, was built in 1799 though perhaps the building was not completed until later as there is a date stone of 1811 above one of the ceilings. The house has extensive cellars of nine rooms which originally contained the kitchen. This was moved upstairs, no doubt for greater convenience, in the 1930s.

Magheralin, about two miles from Lurgan in the direction of Banbridge, lies close to the banks of the River Lagan. The site of the parish church on the right dates from 1842, although the present church was rebuilt in the 1890s having been repaired in 1870. Before the parish church on the right is the former National school dating from 1884 and now used as a youth centre. To its right is the old school master's house, now demolished. The wall which runs down the left hand side conceals a much older churchyard which contains the remains of a church tower built in 1442. In the north wall of the churchyard are thought to be the remains of a monastery founded by St Colman in the seventh century, according to *Bassett's Armagh Directory* of 1888. The stretch of road past the parish church was once called Duck Street after the weavers living there who used duck grease on their looms.

Magheralin village looking towards Lurgan on what is now a busy and much wider main road. This stretch is part of one of the oldest roads in Ireland, the stage coach route to Dublin. Immediately on the left is Byrne's public house which continues in business today on much the same site. Further down on the left is St Patrick's Roman Catholic Church which was built in 1842, a rare example of a Roman Catholic church in Northern Ireland built in a classical style.

Dollingstown, to the east of Lurgan town centre, grew up in the eighteenth century and became an industrial village in the nineteenth. During the twentieth century the Dollingstown Hemstitching Company employed 100 workers and the Lurgan Boxmaking Company there employed 160 workers in the 1960s. Dollingstown was named after Richard Dolling, then owner of the village, whose ancestor the Rev. Boughey William Dolling came to Ireland as Prescentor of Dromore and Rector of Magheralin, another village nearby, in 1806.

A 1930s aerial view of Lurgan, looking over Christ Church. William Street and Lough Road are towards the right while Edward Street is to the left. The fields beyond the church have since disappeared under housing development.

A stretch of Market Street leading to High Street. This photograph dates from the 1950s and shows the Arcade with the large awnings. The Arcade was established as a purveyor of clothing and soft furnishings as early as the 1880s and was a frequent advertiser in the *Lurgan Mail* during the 1900s, but the building was destroyed by a bomb in 1992. Numerous other businesses in the centre of Lurgan were damaged in the same explosion and, as reported in the *Lurgan Mail*, 300 claims for compensation were received by the Northern Ireland Office. Lurgan town centre was also damaged by an earlier explosion in 1983. By the 1950s linen manufacturing in Lurgan had largely declined, but it was still an important shopping centre and remained so until the 1970s when the development of Rushmere at Craigavon Civic Centre drew custom away from Lurgan.

In the 1880s Maghery was a small rural post office about 11 miles from Armagh. It later became a holiday resort with a hotel owing to its attractive situation on the southern shores of Lough Neagh, whose waters it was once believed had curative qualities beneficial to invalids. Close to Maghery is Coney Island which is associated with St Patrick and a sanctuary for wild birds. The River Blackwater joins Lough Neagh here and in 1803 a channel was dug there from the Coalisland Canal so that coal barges could sail the Ulster Canal to Newry and Dublin.